CAMPAIGNED
I ~~Screamed~~
for
ICE CREAM
A BOY'S QUEST FOR ICE CREAM TRUCKS

BY SUZANNE JACOBS LIPSHAW   ILLUSTRATED BY WENDY LEACH

ISBN: 978-1-7339945-0-7 (hard cover)
      978-0-9894814-3-4 (soft cover)
Editing: Amy Ashby

Warren
publishing

Published by Warren Publishing
Charlotte, NC
www.warrenpublishing.net
Printed in the United States

To Josh and Jeremy—my sweetest successes!

On a sizzling summer day, nine-year-old Josh Lipshaw was cheering for his brother Jeremy's tee-ball team when he heard a rare sound—the jingle-jangle of an ice cream truck. Leaping off the bleachers, he grabbed his mom and raced to the truck to buy his favorite ice cream, a chocolate crunch bar.

After gobbling it down, he asked his mom, "Why do ice cream trucks come to Jeremy's tee-ball games, but not our neighborhood?"

"The baseball field's in another town," his mom said. "Ice cream trucks aren't allowed in our town."

Josh was at a loss for words. All he could muster was, "Why?"

"I don't know," she said. "Let's call the township and find out."

Chapter 17
PEDDLERS AND SOLICITORS
ARTICLE I. IN GENERAL

Sec. 17-1 Sales within street
or highway limits.

No person shall, within the limits of any
street or highway within the township,
engage in the sale, barter or exchange
of ice creams, soft drinks, foodstuffs,
fruits, candy, vegetables, flowers, fish bait,
clothing, toys or any other kind of goods,
wares and merchandise, nor engage in any
trade or occupation within such
highway limits.

A few days later, Josh spoke to a clerk at Town Hall who told him ice cream trucks had been banned in West Bloomfield, Michigan due to a 1954 peddler law. This law made it illegal for people to sell anything on city streets—including ice cream!

"That's an old law," Josh said. "And it's not fair other cities get ice cream trucks, but we don't."

Agreeing, the clerk explained the steps Josh could take to change the law.

JOSH COULD HAVE SCREAMED FOR ICE CREAM...

...INSTEAD, HE CAMPAIGNED.

Following instructions from the woman at Town Hall, Josh wrote a letter to the township board of trustees, asking to speak at a meeting. He listed reasons the law should be changed, starting with what he considered a fact—"Everyone likes ice cream!"

Next, Josh searched the internet for a sample petition, a document people sign to show they support a cause, and used it to write his own.

Wanting the trustees to know this was a serious matter, Josh and Jeremy gathered friends to canvass their neighborhood. They went door to door, asking people to sign their petition, and when they were done, they counted 165 signatures!

Josh was on the road to sweet success.

The next day, Josh mailed his letter and petition to the board of trustees and waited...

...and waited...

...and waited.

The exciting news came one week later. Josh was on the agenda to speak at the board's next meeting.

JOSH COULD HAVE SCREAMED FOR ICE CREAM...

Town Hall

Josh Lipshaw

...INSTEAD, HE WROTE A SPEECH.

To prepare, Josh read and reread the law. He asked his parents about their ice cream truck memories. He called neighboring police departments to see if ice cream trucks had caused any safety problems in their cities.

As part of his grassroots effort, Josh passed out flyers to friends, relatives, and neighbors, asking them to support his cause.

When the big day arrived, Josh and his family entered Town Hall. Seeing the audience full of familiar faces, Josh's eyes widened.

He looked at the agenda. Item number six read: "Communication from Joshua Lipshaw regarding ice cream trucks." Head held high, Josh dreamed about summer days filled with frozen treats.

When the board members filed in, Josh's dream of frosty sweets turned into a stream of frosty sweat. Wringing his palms, Josh waited for his turn to speak.

"Item number six," announced the board supervisor.

JOSH COULD HAVE SCREAMED FOR ICE CREAM...

Agenda

1. Operating Budget
2. Public Works – Committee Report
3. Resolution No. 542
4. Expenditure No. 3B
5. Capital Projects Expenditure Ordinance No. 3C
6. Communication from Joshua Lipshaw regarding ice cream trucks

...INSTEAD, HE TOOK A DEEP BREATH AND SPOKE OUT.

"Hello, ladies and gentlemen. I am here today, representing my friends and the kids in our town who would like to have ice cream trucks in the summer."

Josh stated that ice cream trucks should be separated out from the outdated peddler law. He shared that he had called six police departments in neighboring towns and all reported no safety issues involving ice cream trucks. He stressed that no one refused to sign his petition—including adults!

Josh closed with a plea to the trustees, saying, "I bet many of you enjoyed ice cream trucks when you were kids. We deserve the same thing!"

Agenda
1. Operating Budget
2. Public Works - Committee Report
3. Resolution No. 542
4. Expenditure No.
5. Capital Projects Exp
   Ordinance No. 3C
6. Communication from
   Joshua Lipshaw regarding
   ice cream trucks

The audience applauded. Even some board members clapped. When the crowd settled down, the supervisor opened the floor to comments from the community.

A lady spoke first. "I commend Josh for his leadership; however, I hate to be the voice of opposition...."

She disagreed with Josh, stating concerns about children darting into streets, increased litter, and the annoying music.

Josh slumped in his chair.
After more community members spoke, the trustees chimed in.
They debated safety issues.
They discussed the hours drivers could sell ice cream.
They detailed the need for proper licensing for each driver.
The board argued for what seemed like forever.

Finally, the supervisor said, "A motion was made to draft an amendment to allow ice cream trucks. All those in favor say, 'Aye.'"

"Aye," said a chorus of voices.

Josh was on the edge of his seat.

"Any opposed?"

Silence.

"Motion carries."

Josh threw his arms up in victory until…

...a board member said, "We have a procedure we have to follow, and since we have a very young audience here, simply stated, we cannot make a decision tonight."

Two more meetings were needed—one for further discussion and one for the final vote.

Josh's heart sank. He still had an icy road ahead.

One month later, Josh received a draft of the new law entitled "Ordinance to Regulate Frozen Confection Vendors." It sounded so official. Josh's mouth watered as he read on, until one line melted his excitement.

Ice cream trucks couldn't use their bells, chimes, or music.
Josh was stunned. "How would you know if an ice cream truck is coming if you can't hear it?" he asked aloud.

JOSH COULD HAVE SCREAMED FOR ICE CREAM...

...INSTEAD, HE LOBBIED FOR THE BELLS.

At the next meeting, Josh spoke again.
"I am very excited you have made a draft of the ordinance to allow ice cream trucks, but I would like to change one section. Part of the fun of having ice cream trucks is to hear the bells, chimes, and music."
Again, the board members debated...

...and debated...

...and debated.

Finally, the supervisor said, "A motion is on the floor to approve redrafting of the ordinance to allow ice cream trucks to use noisemaking devices. All those in favor say, 'Aye.' ...Opposed?

Motion carries, six to one."
One meeting remained.

JOSH COULD HAVE SCREAMED FOR ICE CREAM...

Wanting more people to know about his mission to lick the ice cream truck ban, Josh gave interviews to two local newspapers.

Suddenly, television stations, radio shows, and more newspapers were calling. Interview requests came from as far off as Toronto, London, and Australia. Josh's story was the hottest scoop around.

At the final meeting, Josh sat frozen in his seat as the supervisor called for the deciding vote.
"All in favor?"
"Aye," said the chorus of voices.
"Any opposed?"
Silence.
The board had unanimously approved the new law!

JOSH COULD HAVE SCREAMED FOR ICE CREAM...

As the crowd cheered, Josh rose to speak one last time.
"I want to thank the township board for listening to a nine-year-old and his friends. You took me seriously, and not everyone would do that. I can't wait to have ice cream trucks this summer!"

On a sunny spring day, Josh heard a rare sound—the jingle-jangle of an ice cream truck. Leaping from the dinner table, he raced outside to see the town's first truck rolling down his street. Josh told the driver about his quest to repeal the ice cream truck ban and the driver thanked him for his hard work.

When Josh went to pay for his chocolate crunch bar, the driver told him to put his money away. Josh's ice cream was free…

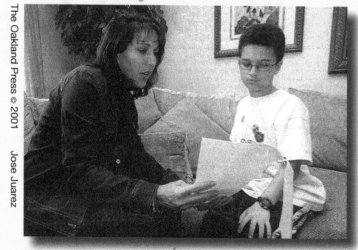

AUTHOR'S NOTE

You may have noticed that Josh and I have the same last name—I am Josh's mom. This story is close to my heart, and I am exceedingly proud of Josh's road to sweet success. His goal was to get ice cream trucks to come to our city. My goal was the same—and more. I wanted Josh to learn about the civic process and to realize anybody has the opportunity, no matter how young or old, to make a difference.

While Josh was "fighting city hall," I was his most enthusiastic cheerleader. To record his story, I put together a scrapbook, which I used to write this book. Included in the scrapbook is a calendar and momentos showing every event of Josh's civic and media adventure. His quest began in July 2001 and went through April 2002.

Many people thought Josh would grow up to be a politician. One journalist even wrote, "And just in case you wondered, he'll be old enough to run for president in, oh…2028." But Josh didn't take that path. Instead, he followed a dream that also dated back to when he was nine—designing spacecraft. Currently, Josh is an aerospace engineer living in Colorado; however, those in West Bloomfield, Michigan still enjoy the benefits of his ice cream campaign every summer!

GLOSSARY

Amendment: a change made to improve something

Board of trustees: an elective board that oversees the decisions of an organization

Campaign: a series of actions carried out to bring an end result

Canvass: to talk to people in an area to get them to support a candidate, project, idea, etc.

Civic: of or relating to a city or town or the people who live there

Confection: a sweet food

Grassroots: the ordinary people in a society or organization

Lobby: a person or group that tries to make lawmakers vote in a certain way

Media: the main means of mass communication, such as newspapers, magazines, TV, radio, and social media

Motion: a formal suggestion or proposal made at a meeting for something to be done

Ordinance: a law or regulation made by a city or town government

Peddler: a person who travels around selling goods that he or she carries from place to place

Petition: a formal request made to a person in authority

Regulate: to enforce a law, rule, or order

Repeal: to officially make a law no longer valid

Supervisor: a person who is in charge of someone or something

Town hall: a town government's main building

Township: a unit of local government in the United States

Trustee: a member of a group that manages an organization

Unanimous: to be fully in agreement

Vendor: a person who sells something